In The Midst of Adversity

A Precis of Job's Life

By Cedieu Leonord

Foreword

Sometimes, life appears a little weird mainly when you face a very unexpected challenge situation. You can even get a point where you ask to yourself about the reason of your presence on the earth. You feel like losing the taste and the meaning of life. And do you know why you have fallen into so much procrastination? Just because you are disappointed and ignore why that happens.

As it can appear in the human life, some situations are much more than what we can see, understand and feel. As human, we experience a lot of situations that are apparently and deeply different. Some of them are clear, others dark. Thus, In the darkest moments of our lives, when trials seem insurmountable and hope wavering, it is natural to seek stories and experiences of courage and faith to guide us. The story of Job, as recorded in the scriptures, is one of those timeless narratives that resonates deeply with those who go through times of great adversity.

Just like us, Job, a man of faith and virtue, according to the Bible, who was subjected to unimaginable trials. In a very special moment of his life, he lost his possessions, his health, and his loved ones, but despite everything, he maintained an unwavering faith in God. This book explores not only Job's suffering, but also his extraordinary resilience and how his faith sustained him through a situation presented and considered as storms of life.

Dear reader, as we delve into each line of this history, we will discover valuable lessons about perseverance, confidence in worse and better days, and the inner strength that are able to allow us overcoming the most daunting obstacles we could face. May this book be a source of inspiration and comfort to all those who seek to find light in moments of darkness.

Summary

According to the Bible, Job was a man living in the land of Uts. He was the father of seven sons and three daughters, and he was the master of many servants.

He is an important and central figure in the Holy Scriptures, known for his unwavering faith and perseverance in the face of extreme trials. Here is a summary of his life:

In his community, Job was a righteous and upright man, wealthy and respected, with a large family and many possessions. One day, Satan defies God by claiming that Job's faithfulness is due to his prosperity. God then allows Satan to test His servant Job, but without taking his life.

Thus, Satan struck Job, and he lost everything like his children, his possessions, and even his health, being struck by painful ulcers. Despite these sufferings, Job refused to curse God. In the meantime, some of his friends like: Eliphaz, Bildad, and Zophar, come to console him but end up accusing him of having sinned to deserve such misfortunes. Job tends to defend his innocence and expresses his confusion and his pain.

Finally, God intervenes, rebukes Job's friends for their unjust accusations. Then He restores Job's prosperity, giving him twice as much wealth as before and new children. Job remains an example of faith and perseverance in the face of adversity.

Table of Contents

Chapter 1

Let us look at some key aspects of Job's life

The life of Job, as described in the Bible, is rich in lessons and profound themes. Here are some key aspects:

Job's piety

Piety is considered as a state of being pious, or devout. it is characterized by a love for God and obedience to His commands and often describes a combination of love and reverence for God.

Job is presented as a man of integrity and uprightness, who loves God and shows respect to Him, and avoids evil. Job did not want to do or say something that could be unpleasant to God. That' s why, he kept faith and didn't deny his faith.

Despite he was a very prosperous man, with a large family and many riches, he remained in the presence of God, following His path and gone out of his way to not offend Him.

Job's piety is a central aspect of his story in the Bible. Job is described as a man of integrity and uprightness, who loves and fears God at a time, and turns away from evil. Here are some key points to explain his piety:

Fear of God

The fear of God is usually used to describe a respectful attitude towards God, rather than outright terror. Therefore, the fear of God can lead to a deep desire to please Him and obey Him, and to avoid disappointing Him.

Let see what he said after receiving the news of death of his children: "Naked *I came from my mother's womb, and naked shall I return. The Lord gave and the Lord has taken away; blessed be the name of the Lord.*" Job 1: 21 What a belief!

Job's fear of God was not a servile fear, but it was a deep respect and reverence for God's power, presence, willing and holiness. This fear had helped him avoiding piously evil and to live according to God's commandments.

Integrity and righteousness

According to the Bible, is considered as a lifestyle of Honesty, moral and consistency. It shows up trust and respect.

Job is presented as a just and honest man, respecting divine and human laws. He is described as "upright and upright" (Job 1:1).

Family devotion

Job shows his piety through his actions towards his family. He consistently offered sacrifices for his children, fearing that they might have sinned and offended God in their hearts (Job 1:5). Thus Job did continually.

Response to suffering

Even when faced with extreme trials, Job maintained his faith and piety. He refuses to curse God despite the loss of his possessions, health, and family, claiming that God gives and takes away (Job 1:21).

Sometimes we offend God with our responses. But God knows that we don't understand and ignore why that happens, sympathizes our weakness and provides us healing.

Dialogue with God

While suffering deeply inside and outside of him, Job engages in an honest dialogue with God, expressing his doubts and sufferings, but never denying his faith. This dialogue shows an authentic and deep relationship with God, based on trust and the search for understanding.

These aspects show that Job's piety is a combination of his moral uprightness, his reverent fear of God, his family devotion, his perseverance in the faith despite trials, and his commitment to sincere dialogue with God.

Do you realize that nothing couldn't separate Job from the love of God?

Job's trials

God has allowed Satan to test Job's faith by inflicting great suffering on him. Satan takes away everything Job owned, including his children.

Job suffered from a painful skin condition called boils that was a great physical agony.

His friends accused him of transgression instead of comforting him.

Do you image that, mostly, people won't hear and understand your cry? Of course, they could not because they are not the ones to talk to when things are going bad. Therefore, God, who knows everything, can hear and understand all your cry, even your tear drops mean to Him. You just need to keep your eyes on Him because He is the hill from where you help will come.

Job loses his children, his possessions, and his health, but he remains faithful to God.

So, don't be afraid, don't give up. God will work it out.

Debates with friends

Job got visited by three of his friends who try to explain his suffering by hidden faults. Job defends his innocence and questions divine justice.

The dialogue between Job and his friends is a central part of the Book of Job in the Bible. After suffering terrible trials, Job expresses his pain and confusion, and his friends Eliphaz, Bildad and Zophar come to console him. However, their exchanges soon become debates about the nature of suffering and divine justice.

Here is a summary of the main dialogues:

First cycle of discourses (Job 4-14):

- Eliphaz, on the other hand, begins by suggesting that Job must have sinned to deserve so much suffering. Job responds by affirming his innocence and expressing his despair.

- Bildad, for his part, insists on God's justice and suggests that Job's children sinned. Job responds by pointing out the apparent injustice of his situation.

- Tsophar, on the other hand, accuses Job of talking too much and not acknowledging his faults. Job continues to defend his innocence and asks God to explain his suffering to him.

Second cycle of discourses (Job 15-21):

- Job's friends repeat their arguments, but with more vehemence. Job, on the other hand, becomes more desperate and critical of God, while maintaining his innocence.

Third cycle of discourse (Job 22-31):

- Eliphaz accuses Job of various specific sins. Job responds by detailing his righteous conduct and asking for an audience with God.

- Bildad and Zophar have shorter interventions, and Job concludes by reaffirming his innocence and expressing his desire to understand the reason for his suffering.

These dialogues show the complexity of the issues of suffering and divine justice, and they highlight Job's unwavering faith despite his trials.

God's response

After hearing the complaining of Job, God finally responds to him from the midst of the storm, emphasizing the complexity and greatness of His wisdom, which is beyond human comprehension.

1. Then the Lord answered Job during the storm. He said:

2. "Who is it that obscures my plans with unconscious words?

3. Prepare yourself like a man; I will question you, and you will answer me.

4. Where were you when I laid the foundation of the earth? Say it if you have intelligence.

5. Who sets the dimensions? Do you know? Who stretched the line over her?

6. On what basis do its foundations rest, or who laid the cornerstone of it,

7. While the morning stars sang together, and all the angels shouted for joy?

8. Who shut up the sea behind gates when it gushed forth from the mother's womb,

9. When I made his garment out of the clouds, and enveloped him in thick darkness,

10. When I set limits on him and set up doors and bolts,

11. When I say, 'You will come here, you will go no further; here will the pride of your waves stop'? (Job 38:1-11, New International Version (NIV))."

These above-mentioned verses show the power, the greatness and the unimaginable wisdom of God as the Creator. Through those lines, He reminds Job and all of us who face a challenging situation that He is great and keeps control on everything He does.

And right after, Job recognizes God's sovereignty and repents of his doubts.

His prosperity

Job's first riches are described in the first chapter of the Book of Job. Again, according to the Bible, Job was a man who feared God and shunned evil. He lived in the land of Uts and had a large family with seven sons and three daughters.

In terms of material wealth, Job possessed:

- 7,000 ewes

- 3,000 camels

- 500 pairs of oxen

- 500 donkeys

- Many minions

These possessions made him one of the richest and most respected men in his community and in the East.

Chapter 2
Why did God allow satan to test Job's faith?

God allowed Satan to assess Job's faith for several important reasons:

Testing the sincerity of Job's faith

Satan claimed that Job's faithfulness was solely due to his material blessings. By allowing Satan to test Job, God demonstrated that Job's faith was genuine and not based on his possessions.

The end of this experience proves that God was right.

Please, let me ask you this question: Can the almighty count on you in good or bad times?

Showing human loyalty

In the Bible, loyalty is described as a commitment to God, to people and to righteous causes. Other times, it is described as a way to live generously.

God wanted to prove that humans can remain faithful even in the worst trials. Job showed unwavering faith despite his sufferings. I believe that you can do it too.

Glorifying God

It looks contradictory and controverse that God can be glorified while we suffer!

Let's take on what is written in 1 Peter 4: 14 – 16 : " *If you are insulted for the name of Christ, you are blessed because the Spirit of Glory rests upon you. But, let none of you suffer as a murderer or a thief or an evildoer or as a meddler. Yet, if anyone suffers as a Christian, let him not be ashamed, but let him glorify God in that name.* "

Through Job's trials, God was finally glorified because he kept faith. In Job chapter 1 verse 20, after receiving the broken news about his possessions and his progeniture, Jog arose and tore his robe. He shaved his head and fell on the ground to worship God. What a man! what a grace! what a resilience! What a faith! In despite of all, Job recognized God's sovereignty and wisdom, even in unconceivable suffering.

It is written in 1 Peter 1:7: "... so that the trial of your faith, more precious than perishable gold (which, however, tried by fire), may result in praise, glory, and honor, when Jesus appears. »

Teaching Spiritual Lessons

Suffering is the feeling of moral or physical pain.

It is synonymous with affliction, injury, pain, sorrow, torment, heartbreak, etc.

Here are some examples of what Scripture says to this effect:

o *James 1:2-3: "My brethren, consider as a matter of complete joy the various trials to which you may be exposed, knowing that the trial of your faith produces patience."*

o *Job 36:15: "But God saves the poor in his misery, and by suffering He warns him."*

o *Psalm 107:12: "He humbled their hearts with suffering; they succumbed, and no one helped them. In their distress they cried out to the Lord and He delivered them from their anguish. »*

o *Hebrews 5:7-8: "It is he who in the days of his flesh, having cried out and wept prayers and supplications to him who could save him from death, and having been heard because of his godliness, learned, though he was a Son, obedience by the things which he suffered."*

The story of Job offers profound lessons about suffering, faith, and divine justice. It shows that suffering is not always a punishment for sin but can be a test of faith.

That's why you need to be vigilant as a servant of the Lord.

These reasons show that Job's trials had a greater purpose, beyond mere suffering, and served to demonstrate the depth of faith and divine justice.

Chapter 3

Specific lessons we can learn from the story of Job

The story of Job in the Bible offers several valuable and useful teachings. Here are some specific lessons we can learn from this:

Faithfulness in adversity

When the dark moments appear, and you see where to go nor what to do, look at Job's experience and keep faith.

Job remained faithful to God despite his extreme suffering. It teaches us the importance of maintaining our faith even in the most tough times.

Please look at Job 2:10

God's Sovereignty

God is sovereign and His ways are beyond our human comprehension. He exercices His power according His willing. He does whatever He want, everywhere, anyhow. Job understood that. Thet way of his life teaches us to accept that some things are beyond and above our own comprehension.

In Job 37:23: "We cannot come to the Almighty, Great by force, by righteousness, by sovereign right: He does not answer! "

The Value of Integrity

Job is described as a man of integrity and uprightness. His story underscores the importance of integrity and righteousness, even when we face trials. (Job 1:1)

In Job 8:20, it is recorded, "No, God does not reject the upright man, nor does He protect the wicked." Therefore, the one who walks in integrity is of excellent value in the sight of God.

Support and compassion!

Sometimes, you may be surprised and deceived by the attitude of those around you. This is why support and compassion are important to be cultivated.

Job's friends come to console him, but they end up criticizing him. This shows the importance of supporting and showing compassion to those who are suffering, without judging them.

Patience and endurance

Job shows great patience and endurance in the face of his trials. It reminds us that patience is an essential virtue in life.

The Bible says, "Behold, blessed are those who have suffered patiently. You have heard of Job's suffering, and you have seen the end that the Lord gave him because the Lord is full of mercy and compassion. James 5:11

"Is any of you suffering? Let him pray. Is any of you rejoicing? Let him sing hymns. James 5:13. Alleluia!

Keep faith, for it is this virtue that will lead you to patience and strengthen you enough to get through the challenging times of life.

Chapter 4
Specific verses in the Bible related to the story of Job

Several key verses in the Bible are related to the story of Job. Here are some of the most significant:

1. **Job 1:1** *"There was a man in the land of Uz whose name was Job. This man was upright and upright; he feared God and turned away from evil." This verse introduces Job as a righteous and pious man.*

2. *Job 1:21: "He said, 'I came out naked from my mother's womb, and naked I will return to the bosom of the earth. The Lord gave, and the Lord took away; blessed be the name of the Lord!'" Job here expresses his faith and submission to God's will, even after he had lost everything he owned.*

3. *Job 2:10: "But Job answered him, 'You speak like a foolish woman. What! we receive good from God, and we would not also receive evil!' In all this Job did not sin with his lips." This verse shows Job's faithfulness despite his wife's advice to curse God.*

4. *Job 13:15: "Behold, he will kill me; I have nothing to hope for, but I will defend my conduct before him." Here Job expresses his determination to remain faithful to God, even in the face of death.*

*5. **Job 19:25-26:** "But I know that my Redeemer lives, and that he will rise last on the earth. When my skin is destroyed, he will rise; when I have no more flesh, I will see God."* Job expresses his faith in the resurrection and in divine justice.

These verses illustrate the depth of Job's faith and the spiritual lessons we can learn from his story.

Chapter 5
Did not Job's friends love him?

Job's friends, although they made mistakes in their approach, did not lack love for him. Their presence in this special moment is very significant.

Here are a few things to consider:

Their original intention

Job's friends, Eliphaz, Bildad and Zophar, came from everywhere to console him and support him in his suffering. This shows that they cared about him and wanted to help him. So, they acted in good faith.

Their presence

They spent seven days and nights in silence with Job, sharing his pain without saying a word. This period of silence shows their respect and compassion for his suffering.

In this moment of silence, their presence speaks extremely loudly.

Their mistakes

Although they tried to console Job, they made erroneous assumptions about the cause of his sufferings, believing that they were due to hidden sins.

Their theology of divine retribution led them to falsely accuse Job.

For example, Eliphaz of Teman spoke up and said: "Search in your memory: Who and the innocent one who perished? Who are the righteous who have been exterminated? As for me, I have seen, those who plough iniquity and sow injustice reap its fruits. Job 4:7-8

Eliphaz, one of his friends, wanted to strengthen him, but his intervention was not according to God's will. Therefore, it is good to avoid hasty conclusions if one has not received any revelation from God, Lord of heaven and earth.

Their love is poorly expressed

Despite their mistakes, their intentions were to do well. They wanted to help Job understand and overcome his trials, even if their counsel was misguided.

In short, Job's friends loved him, but their limited understanding of suffering and divine justice led them to erroneous conclusions. Their story reminds us of the importance of compassion and attentive listening without judgment.

Chapter 6
Other lessons we can learn from the mistakes of Job's friends

The mistakes of Job's friends offer several important lessons about how to support someone who is suffering. Here are some of the key lessons:

Avoid hasty judgments

Job's friends quickly concluded that his suffering was due to hidden sins. Today, it is easy to find people acting the same way, ready to judge others without knowing the who story. Remember support and compassion.

It is not wise to judge other on a situation that he faces. Our God doesn't want that.

Listen with compassion

At first, Job's friends showed compassion by remaining silent with him for seven days. However, they then began to accuse him.

It is crucial to listen with empathy and show compassion without judgment.

We have limit

Job's friends have been trying to explain Job's suffering using their own limited understanding. They couldn't perceive the hand of God in this situation and risked facing the divine justice.

This mistake teaches and reminds us that we do not always understand God's plans and that we need to be humble in our counsels, speeches and actions. Recognize our weakness and limit.

Offer unconditional support

Instead of criticizing, it is important to support our friends unconditionally. Jesus has left this commandment: *"love one another. as I have loved you, so you most love one another. By this, all men will know that you are my disciples, if you love one another. "* John 13: 34-35

Job's friends could have supported him better by offering their presence and love without trying to find explanations.

Do not speak in the name of God without certainty

Job's friends claimed to know God's will, which added to Job's suffering. We must be careful when speaking in God's name and avoid making definitive statements about His intentions. It is good form to think before speaking in the name of God.

Encouraging patience and faith

Rather than criticizing, we should encourage those who are suffering to keep the faith and be patient, reminding them that God is with them even in challenging times.

These lessons help us better understand how to provide true and compassionate support to those who are going through hardships.

Chapter 7
Did Job love his wife

The Bible does not give many explicit details about the relationship between Job and his wife, but there are a few things that can help us understand their dynamics:

Attendance and initial support

Job and his wife went through extremely difficult trials together. She stayed by his side during his suffering, which shows a certain level of support and presence.

Job's reaction to his wife

When his wife told him to "curse God and die" (Job 2:9), Job responded by saying that she was talking like a foolish woman, but he did not reject or abandon her. This may indicate that he had affection for her despite their disagreement.

In summary, although the Bible does not provide explicit details about Job's love for his wife, the available evidence suggests that he had affection and respect for her, even in times of disagreement and suffering.

Chapter 8
Why did job's wife say thus?

Job's wife spoke this way for several reasons, reflecting her own suffering and despair:

Despair and suffering

She had lost her children, her possessions, and saw her husband suffering terribly. Going through this situation was not easy for her. His advice to "curse God and die" can be seen as an expression of his own desperation and intense pain.

Perception of injustice

She could perceive the situation as a divine injustice. Seeing Job, a righteous man, suffer for no apparent reason, she may have thought that God had abandoned them.

Satan's influence

Some biblical commentators suggest that Satan used Job's wife to tempt Job to renounce his faith. Satan had spared Job's wife so that she could be an instrument of temptation during these times of pain.

Lack of understanding

Like Job's friends, she may have had a limited understanding of suffering and divine justice. She did not see God's greater plan behind Job's trials.

These reasons show that Job's wife's reaction was complex and influenced by many emotional and spiritual factors.

Chapter 9
How did Job react to his wife's words

When Job's wife told him to "curse God and die" (Job 2:9), Job responded with a gentle but firm rebuke. He said, "You talk like a foolish woman. What! we receive good from God, and we would not also receive evil?" (Job 2:10) With this response, Job showed his determination to remain faithful to God, even in times of great suffering.

Job recognized that life has both blessings and trials, and he chose to accept both with faith and resilience. His reaction shows his deep confidence in God's sovereignty and justice, despite the difficult circumstances.

Chapter 10
What other reactions of job are significant in the story?

Job had several significant reactions throughout his history, which illustrate his faith, patience, and resilience. Here are some of the most memorable:

Initial acceptance of suffering

After losing his children and possessions, Job said, "The Lord has given, and the Lord has taken away; blessed be the name of the Lord!" (Job 1:21) This reaction shows his submission and his unwavering faith in God.

Refusal to sin with his lips

Even after being covered with plagues, Job refused to sin in words against God. "In all these things Job did not sin with his lips" (Job 2:10). This demonstrates his determination to remain faithful.

Expressing pain and questions

Job did not hide his suffering. He expressed his pain and questions to God, showing that it is okay to seek answers and share one's feelings with God (Job 3:1-26).

Defending his innocence

Job defended his innocence in the face of his friends' accusations, claiming that he had not committed a sin to deserve his sufferings: "Far be it from me to agree with you! Until my last breath I will defend my innocence. I want to justify myself and I will not falter. My heart does not reproach me for any of my days. (Job 27:5-6). What assurance! This shows his integrity and confidence in his own righteousness.

Acknowledging God's sovereignty

After God spoke to him, Job recognized God's greatness and wisdom, saying, "I know that you can do all things, and that nothing stands in the way of your thoughts" (Job 42:2). This reaction shows his humility and submission to the divine will.

Intercession for his friends

At the end of the story, Job prayed for his friends, and God accepted his prayer and forgave them (Job 42:10). This shows his ability to forgive and intercede for others.

These reactions of Job offer us valuable lessons about faith, patience, and how to deal with suffering.

Chapter 11
Specific verses from the book of Job

We can identify several verses in the book of Job that are particularly striking and offer profound lessons. Here are some of the most significant:

1.   Job 1:21

"The Lord gave, and the Lord took away; blessed be the name of the Lord!" This verse shows Job's unwavering faith despite his immense losses.

2.   Job 2:10

"You talk like a foolish woman. What! we receive good from God, and we would not also receive evil?" Job reminds us here of the importance of accepting both the blessings and the trials of life.

3.   Job 13:15

"Behold, he will kill me; I have nothing to hope for, but I will defend my conduct before him." This verse illustrates Job's determination to remain faithful and defend his innocence.

4.   Job 19:25-26

"But I know that my redeemer lives, and that he will rise last on the earth. When my skin is destroyed, he will rise; when I have no more flesh, I will see God." Job expresses here his faith in the resurrection and in divine justice.

5.   Job 42:2

"I recognize that you can do anything, and that nothing stands in the way of your thoughts." After hearing God, Job recognizes God's sovereignty and omnipotence.

These verses are powerful and offer profound insights into faith, suffering, and divine justice.

Chapter 12
When did God allow satan to test job?

God allowed Satan to test Job at a heavenly meeting where the "sons of God" appeared before the Lord. Satan came among them, and God called Satan's attention to Job, a man of integrity and righteousness. Satan then challenged Job's faithfulness, claiming that he was faithful only because he was blessed. So, God allowed Satan to test Job to prove the sincerity of his faith.

Here is the key passage from Job 1:6-12:

- Job 1:6-8: "Now the sons of God came one day to present themselves before the LORD, and Satan also came among them. The Lord said to Satan, 'Where do you come from?' And Satan answered the LORD, 'To walk the earth and walk on it.' The Lord said to Satan, 'Have you noticed my servant, Job? There is no one like him on earth; he is a man of integrity and uprightness, fearing God, and turning away from evil.'"

- Job 1:9-12: "And Satan answered the Lord, 'Is Job selflessly fearing God? Have you not protected him, his house, and all that is his? You have blessed the work of his hands, and his flocks cover the land. But stretch out your hand, touch everything that belongs to him, and I am sure he will curse you to your face.'

The Lord said to Satan, 'Behold, all that belongs to him I deliver to you; only do not lay your hand on him. And Satan departed from before the face of the LORD."

This passage shows how God allowed Satan to test Job in order to demonstrate the depth of his faith and faithfulness.

Chapter 13
Wasn't there another way to test Job's faith?

The question of whether there was another way to test Job's faith is complex. In the biblical context, God chose to allow Satan to test Job through suffering for several specific reasons, such as demonstrating the sincerity of Job's faith and teaching profound spiritual lessons. However, there are other ways in which God can test the faith of individuals, as shown by other biblical accounts and spiritual teachings:

New challenges

A new challenge can be extremely beneficial in someone's life for several reasons:

1. Building resilience: Overcoming obstacles strengthens the ability to manage stress and difficulties, making a person more resilient to future challenges.

2. Increased self-confidence: Succeeding in a challenge, even a small one, can significantly increase self-confidence and a sense of accomplishment.

3- Personal growth: Facing new challenges pushes you out of your comfort zone, which promotes the development of new skills and the acquisition of knowledge.

4. Discovering New Passions: By trying something new, one can discover hidden interests or talents that could become new passions or careers.

5. Improved mental health: Challenges can bring a sense of purpose and motivation, which is beneficial for mental health and overall well-being.

In turn, God can test our faith by giving us difficult tasks and/or missions that seem impossible, such as when He asked Noah to build the ark.

Major changes

Significant life changes, such as a move or career change, can also be tests of faith, as was the case for Abraham when he was called to leave his country without knowing where he was going.

Delayed promises

Waiting for the fulfillment of God's promises can be a test of faith, just as Abraham and Sarah had to wait a long time for the birth of their son Isaac.

Prolongation of pain

Living with prolonged pain or suffering, whether physical, emotional, or spiritual, can also test our faith and endurance. We come out of one pain to another, from one difficult moment to another, etc. ...; God remains.

These examples show that God uses a variety of methods to test and strengthen our faith. In Job's case, extreme suffering was the chosen means to demonstrate the depth of his faith and to teach important lessons about divine justice and faithfulness.

Chapter 14
Specific teachings on suffering and faithfulness

There are many inspiring teachings about suffering and faithfulness through the Bible and theological commentaries. Here are some of the most memorable:

Suffering is not always a punishment

The story of Job shows that suffering is not necessarily the result of personal sin. Job was a righteous man, and his trials served to demonstrate the depth of his faith.

Faithfulness in adversity

Job maintained his faith in God despite immense losses and intense suffering. It teaches us the importance of staying true even in the most tough times.

God's sovereignty

Job learned that God's ways are beyond human comprehension.

In his answer to Job, God asks, "Who is it that obscures my purposes with unintelligent speeches?" (Job 38:2)

He continues in Job 40:2: "Is he who disputes against the Almighty convinced? Does he who disputes with God have a reply to make? (Job 40:2)

And Job answered and said, "Behold, I am too little, what shall I say to you? I put my hand over my mouth. (Job 40:4)

It reminds us to trust in God's wisdom and sovereignty, even when we do not understand our circumstances.

Personal growth

Suffering can be a means of personal and spiritual growth. Job emerged from his trials with a deeper faith and a greater understanding of God. He says, "I acknowledge that you can do all things, and that nothing stands in the way of your thoughts." Job 42:2

Support from others

Although Job's friends made mistakes, their initial presence shows the importance of supporting those who are suffering. We must be there for our loved ones in their moments of need.

Chapter 15
Transformed after being tested

After all his suffering, Job did not remain the same, but he emerged with a deeper faith and understanding of God. Here are some key points about Job's transformation:

Strengthened faith

Despite his trials, Job remained loyal to God and refused to curse Him. Her faith was tested, but she came out stronger.

Increased understand of God

At the end of his trials, Job had a direct encounter with God, who revealed to him the greatness and complexity of His plans. Job recognized God's sovereignty and understood that some things are beyond human comprehension (Job 42:1-6).

Humility and repentance

Job expressed humility and repentance after hearing God. He said, "I know that you can do all things, and that nothing stands in the way of your thoughts" (Job 42:2). This shows that he has gained a new perspective on his own place in the universe.

Restoration and blessings

God restored Job, giving him twice as much wealth as before and blessing his family. Job lived a long and prosperous life after his trials, which shows that his faithfulness was rewarded.

In summary, although Job went through intense suffering, he came out of it transformed, with a deeper faith and a heightened understanding of God's sovereignty.

Chapter 16
How did satan proceed to inflict suffering on Job?

Satan proceeded methodically to inflict suffering on Job, in several stages, after receiving God's permission. Here is how it went:

Destruction of Job's goods and servants

Satan began by attacking Job's material possessions. He incited the Sabaeans to steal Job's oxen and donkeys and kill his servants (Job 1:14-15). Then he brought down fire from heaven that burned the sheep and the servants (Job 1:16).

Attack on Job's children

Satan then caused a great storm that caused the house where Job's children were celebrating to collapse, killing them all (Job 1:18-19).

Physical affliction

After destroying Job's property and family, Satan was given permission to touch his body. He then struck Job with painful wounds from head to foot (Job 2:7).

Isolation and despair

In addition to physical suffering, Satan used Job's wife to try to get him to curse God and die (Job 2:9). Job's friends, who came to console him, finally added to his suffering by falsely accusing him.

These steps show how Satan used successive and varied attacks to test Job's faith and resilience. Despite these trials, Job remained faithful to God, demonstrating the depth of his faith.

Chapter 17
Is God not complicit in Job's suffering?

The question of God's complicity in Job's sufferings is complex and has been debated by many theologians. Here are some key points to consider:

God allows but does not initiate

In the book of Job, God allows Satan to test Job, but He is not the direct initiator of suffering. God allowed these trials to demonstrate the sincerity of Job's faith and to teach profound spiritual lessons.

Sovereignty and divine justice

God sometimes uses suffering to accomplish greater goals than we can comprehend. Job's suffering served to demonstrate the depth of his faith and to offer lessons in divine justice and faithfulness.

God is not cruel

The book of Job shows that God is neither cruel nor vindictive. Rather, God is described as "merciful and compassionate, slow to anger, and abounding in kindness and faithfulness" (Exodus 34:6). Job's suffering was not a punishment for a sin, but a test of faith.

Chapter 18
God's response to Job

When God responds to Job, He does not give a detailed justification for suffering, but He emphasizes the greatness and complexity of His plans, which are beyond human comprehension. Job acknowledges God's sovereignty and repents of his doubts (Job 42:1-6).

In summary, although God allowed Job's suffering, He did so for a greater purpose, demonstrating the depth of Job's faith and teaching important lessons about divine justice and faithfulness.

Chapter 19
To find peace and hope in times of suffering

Finding peace and hope in times of suffering can be a challenge, but there are several ways to do it:

Prayer and meditation

Spend time in prayer and meditation. Talk to God about your suffering and ask Him to give you peace and strength. Prayer can bring great comfort and a deeper connection with God.

Reading the scriptures

Bible verses can offer immense comfort. For example, Matthew 11:28-30 says, "Come to me, all you who are weary and heavy laden, and I will give you rest. Take my yoke upon you and receive my instructions, for I am meek and humble of heart; and you will find rest for your souls. For my yoke is easy, and my burden is light."

Community and support

Surround yourself with people who can support you. Talking to friends, family members, or spiritual advisors can help you carry your burdens and find comfort.

Acceptance and resilience

Accept that suffering is a part of life and can be an opportunity for personal and spiritual growth. As James 1:2-4 says: "My brethren, consider the various trials to which you may be exposed as a matter of complete joy, knowing that the trial of your faith produces patience."

Calming activities

Engage in activities that bring you peace, such as reading, listening to soothing music, walking in nature, or practicing mindfulness.

Perspective and hope

Remember that suffering is not eternal, and God has a plan for you. Romans 8:28 says, "We know, moreover, that all things work together for good to those who love God, to those who are called according to his purpose."

These practices can help you find peace and hope even in the most challenging times.

Chapter 20
Was this period of suffering part of God's plan for Job?

Job's period of suffering is part of a larger plan by God, although the precise reasons are not fully explained in the biblical text. Here are some key points to consider:

Job's faith test

God allowed Satan to test Job to demonstrate the sincerity of his faith. Satan claimed that Job was faithful only because of his material blessings, and God allowed these trials to prove that Job's faith was genuine.

Revelation of god's sovereignty

Through Job's sufferings, God revealed His sovereignty and wisdom. Job learned that God's ways are beyond human comprehension and that he must trust in God's wisdom.

Spiritual lessons

The story of Job offers profound lessons about suffering, faith, and divine justice. It shows that suffering is not always a punishment for sin but can be a test of faith and a means of spiritual growth.

Chapter 21
Before his period of suffering, Job was extremely prosperous and respected. Here is a look at he owned

Extended family

Job had ten children, seven sons and three daughters (Job 1:2).

Material wealth

He owned vast quantities of livestock, including 7,000 sheep, 3,000 camels, five hundred pairs of oxen, and five hundred donkeys (Job 1:3). These possessions made him one of the richest men in the East.

Servants

Job had many servants to manage his possessions and lands (Job 1:3).

Respect and influence

Job was highly respected in his community for his uprightness and integrity. He was considered a man of integrity and righteousness, fearing God, and turning away from evil (Job 1:1).

These possessions and his status show how prosperous Job was before the trials began.

Chapter 22
What lessons can we learn from Job's material losses?

Job's material losses offer several important lessons about faith, resilience, and spiritual perspective. Here are some of the key lessons:

The value of faith independent of possessions

Job showed that his faith in God was not based on his material possessions. Even after he had lost everything, he said, "The Lord has given, and the Lord has taken away; blessed be the name of the Lord!" (Job 1:21) This teaches us that our faith must be anchored in God, regardless of our material circumstances.

The importance of resilience

Job showed remarkable resilience in the face of immense losses. His ability to continue to worship God despite his suffering shows the importance of perseverance and resilience in faith.

The recognition of God sovereignty

Job recognized that God is sovereign and that everything he possessed came from Him. This perspective reminds us that everything we have is a gift from God and that we must be willing to accept both blessings and trials.

Transformation through suffering

Job's trials led to a profound spiritual transformation. He gained a deeper understanding of God's sovereignty and wisdom, which strengthened his faith and humility (Job 42:1-6).

Chapter 23
Restoration and blessing

At the end of the story, God restored Job and gave him blessings beyond his initial losses. This shows that faithfulness and perseverance can lead to unimaginable blessings and restoration, even after times of great suffering.

James 1:12: "Blessed is the man who patiently endures temptation; for, after he has been tried, he will receive the crown of life, which the Lord has promised to those who love him."

These lessons offer us profound perspectives on how to deal with material losses and maintain our faith in God.

Chapter 24
What was Job like during times of suffering

During his times of suffering, Job showed remarkable faith and resilience, despite extremely difficult trials. Here are some aspects of his behavior and reactions:

Initial acceptance

After losing his children and possessions, Job expressed his faith by saying, "The Lord has given, and the Lord has taken away; blessed be the name of the Lord!" (Job 1:21) He accepted his losses with an attitude of submission to God's will.

Refusal to sin

Sin can get you far from the presence of God. It is considered as an act of transgression against divine law.

So, even after being struck with painful wounds, Job refused to sin in words against God. He replied to his wife, "You talk like a foolish woman. What! we receive good from God, and we would not also receive evil?" (Job 2:10) Job had the determination to remain faithful. Is not that wonderful!

Find yourself a reason to flee sin.

Expression of his pain

Expressing is a great opportunity to communicate your thoughts, your feelings, your needs, your belief and so on.

Job did not hide his suffering. He expressed his pain and questions to God, wondering why he was enduring so much pain (Job 3:1-26). He also had to deal with accusations from his friends, who believed that his suffering was a punishment for a hidden sin.

Defending his innocence

In the face of accusations from his friends, Job defended his innocence, claiming that he had not committed sin to deserve his suffering (Job 27:5-6). He has reacted that way because of his integrity and confidence in his own righteousness. Be honest!

Acknowledging God's sovereignty

After God spoke to him, Job recognized God's greatness and wisdom, saying, "I know that you can do all things, and that nothing stands in the way of your thoughts" (Job 42:2). This reaction shows his humility and submission to the divine will. Of course, you can do the same.

Intercession for his friends

At the end of the story, Job prayed for his friends, and God accepted his prayer and forgave them (Job 42:10). This shows his ability to forgive and intercede for others.

These reactions of Job illustrate his unwavering faith, patience, and resilience in the face of extreme trials.

Chapter 25
How can I apply job's faith and resilience to my own life?

Applying Job's faith and resilience to your own life can help you get through challenging times with courage and hope. Here are some practical steps to achieve this:

Embracing resilience in adversity

To achieve this, like Job, try to stay strong and not lose hope even when you face challenges. Consider that life is made of challenges. For you are alive, you must face them. And resilience is useful tool that can help you to overcome hardships and come out stronger. So, a better version of you might become exposed.

Trusting in divine wisdom

Believe in God is a virtue. It is also a powerful strength for those who want and decide to walk in the paths of God. You need to keep it strongly if would like to be victorious.

Job maintained his trust in God even when he did not understand his suffering. Believe that God has a plan for you, even if the circumstances seem incomprehensible.

Practice patience

Patience is key to getting through tough times. It is a capacity that allows you to accept suffering and trouble without getting angry. When you are patient, you have the ability to wait, to follow the process without complaining. Job showed remarkable patience, which allowed him to endure his trials without losing his faith.

Avoiding hasty judgments

Like Job's friends, we may be tempted to quickly judge the situations of others. Remember that the purpose of God of putting us together is not to judge nor condemn others, but to love each other. Use our mouth to bless, not to hurt. Try to offer compassion and support in a non-judgmental way.

Finding gratitude during loss

Gratitude is a quality of being thankful. Even in his suffering, Job found reason to be grateful. He did not forget the glory and the kindness of God. Do not let a situation change your personality. Be grateful for everything, every day and everywhere. Cultivating a grateful heart can help you see blessings even in challenging times.

Accept incertitude

Life is full of uncertainty, and Job has learned to accept this. That can seem unbelievable, but it is true. Accept that some things are out of your control, and trust God to guide you. Do not force anything, let God lead the boat because He knows the best destination for you.

Prayer and meditation

Spend time in prayer and meditation to strengthen your connection with God. Prayer can bring great peace and a renewed perspective.

By incorporating these practices into your daily life, you can develop Job-like faith and resilience, helping you get through tough times with grace and courage.

Chapter 26
What made Job resist?

Job was able to withstand his trials thanks to several key factors:

Deep faith in God

Job's unwavering faith in God was the foundation of his resilience. He passionately believed in God's sovereignty and justice, even when he did not understand the reasons for his sufferings (Job 1:21; Job 2:10).

Personal integrity

Job was a man of integrity and uprightness. His clear conscience and commitment to righteousness helped him stay true to his principles, even in the face of accusations from his friends (Job 27:5-6).

Patience and endurance

Job showed remarkable patience. He bore his trials with an endurance that allowed him not to lose hope, even in the darkest moments (James 5:11).

Expressing your emotions

Job did not repress his feelings. He expressed his pain, questions, and frustrations to God, which allowed him to release his emotions and seek answers (Job 3:1-26). But he did not offense god.

Don't be afraid to express your feelings, or your thoughts when it is necessary. But, overall, be true, honest and sincere.

Community support

Our community is very important to us. That's why God desires that his beloved children support and pray for one another.

Although his friends made mistakes, their initial presence and intention to console him show the importance of community support. In the end, Job also received support from his family and friends (Job 42:11).

Surround yourself with people who can support you. Sharing your burdens with friends, family, or spiritual advisors can bring you comfort and strength.

Divine revelation

Job's direct encounter with God was a turning point. God revealed to him the greatness and complexity of His plans, which strengthened Job's faith and gave him a new perspective (Job 42:1-6). He became stronger than ever.

These combined elements enabled Job to withstand his trials and emerge from his suffering with a deeper faith and understanding of the almighty God.

Chapter 27
Towards restoration

God restored Job significantly and completely after his trials because he was victorious. In despite of all, he did not lose faith.

Here is how it went:

Prayer for friends

Job's restoration began after he prayed for his friends. God asked Job to pray for them, and when he did, God began to restore his fortunes (Job 42:10).

When you pray for others, that allows you to be closer of them and love them. Whether you were frustrated because of their attitude, praying for them helps you forgive, pardon and do not focus on their weakness. Praying for others strengthens our relationship between us, beautify our moments keeps us closer to God.

Forgive and go ahead. The followings-up are surprising.

Double blessing

God gave Job twice as much as he had before his trials. Job received 14,000 sheep, 6,000 camels, 1,000 pairs of oxen, and 1,000 donkeys, doubling his initial possessions (Job 42:12).

New family

Job had new children, seven sons and three daughters. His daughters were especially notable for their beauty, and Job gave them a share of the inheritance among their brothers, which was unusual at the time (Job 42:13-15).

Long life and prosperity

Job lived another 140 years after his trials, seeing his children and grandchildren up to the fourth generation. He died old and full of days, which indicates a long and prosperous life (Job 42:16-17).

Consolation and support

Job's brothers, sisters, and old friends came to console and support him. They shared a meal with him and gave him silver and gold rings, showing their support and reconciliation (Job 42:11).

These actions show how God not only restored Job's material possessions, but also gave him a new family, a long life, and the support of his community. Job's restoration is a powerful testimony of God's faithfulness and the reward of faith and perseverance.

Chapter 28
Some other ways that can help you deepen your faith

There are many ways to deepen your faith. Here are some practical suggestions:

Regular Prayer

Spend time each day in prayer. Talk to God about your concerns, thank Him for His blessings, and ask Him to guide you.

Bible Study

Read and ponder the scriptures regularly. Try to understand the context and teachings of the passages you are reading.

Community

Join a prayer group or religious community. Sharing your faith with others can encourage and support you.

Service to others

Engage in volunteer or service activities. Helping others can strengthen your faith and bring you closer to God.

Gratitude

Practice gratitude by writing down the things you are grateful for each day. It can help you see God's hand in your daily life.

Patience and trust

Learn to trust God in challenging times. Patience and trust in His plans can strengthen your faith.

Spiritual Reading

Read books or articles about faith and spirituality. This can provide you with new perspectives and deepen your understanding.

Personal reflection

Take time to reflect on your life and your relationship with God. Meditation and reflection can help you see how God works in your life.

Participation in the sacraments

Participate regularly in your church's sacraments, such as communion. This can strengthen your spiritual connection.

Music and praise

Listen to spiritual music and participate in worship moments. Music can be a powerful source of inspiration and connection with God.

By incorporating these practices into your daily life, you can deepen your faith and strengthen your relationship with God.

Chapter 29
Bible verses that talk about compassion and support for others

Here are some Bible verses that talk about compassion and support for others:

1.   Ephesians 4:32

"Be kind to one another, compassionate, forgiving one another, as God has forgiven you in Christ."

2. Psalm 145:8

"The Lord is merciful and compassionate, slow to anger and full of kindness."

1.   1 Peter 3:8

"Finally, be all animated by the same thoughts and feelings, full of fraternal love, compassion, humility."

1.   1 Thessalonians 5 :11

"Therefore exhort one another, and edify one another, as in reality you do."

1.   Acts 20:35

"I have shown you in every way that it is by working in this way that you must support the weak, and remember the words of the Lord, who himself said: 'It is more blessed to give than to receive'.

These verses emphasize the importance of compassion and mutual support in the Christian faith.

Bibliography

Some Commentaries and Meditations on the Book of Job

Several commentaries and meditations on the book of Job are particularly striking and offer profound perspectives. Here are some examples:

1. Timeless Lessons from the Book of Job: This commentary emphasizes that the Book of Job helps Christians to suffer well, by allowing them to trust God even in times of suffering. It emphasizes God's sovereignty and the importance of faith and patience.

2. Top 5 Commentaries on the Book of Job: This guide features the best comments on Job, including those from David J. A. Clines and John Hartley. These commentaries offer in-depth analyses and theological perspectives on the text, helping readers to understand the completeness of the book of Job.

3. Enduring Word Bible Commentary: David Guzik offers a detailed commentary on Job, highlighting the themes of suffering, divine justice, and faith. His approachable approach helps readers apply Job's lessons to their own lives.

These resources offer meditations and analysis that can enrich your understanding of the book of Job and help you learn profound spiritual lessons.

Bible Gateway

God Restores Job's Fortunes - Bible Gateway

God And the Restoration of His Wealth (Bible Stories Explained0.

How Does God Restore Us? | Job 42:10 | Daily Devotion | Daily Bible Verse

The Book of Job (Biblical Stories Explained)

You version (Bible)

12 Reasons Why God Restored the Prosperity of Job

Job 42:10 After Job had prayed for his friends, the LORD restored his ....

Job, an example of perseverance for the Christian (James 5:7-11).

The Book of Job: Why the Righteous Are Confronted with Evil...

The Book of Job - Hozana.

Job (biblical character) - Vikidia, the encyclopedia for 8–13-year-olds.

The Seven Lessons of Job's Story

www.ingramcontent.com/pod-product-compliance
Lightning Source LLC
Chambersburg PA
CBHW051330120626
46547CB00016B/2480